# Samples from this book

Copyright © 2019 by Ashley's Notebooks

All rights reserved. No part of this publication may be reproduced, distributed, or transmitted in any form or by any means, including photocopying, recording, or other electronic or mechanical methods, without the prior written permission of the publisher, except in the case of brief quotations embodied in critical reviews and certain other noncommercial uses permitted by copyright law. For permission requests, write to the publisher, addressed "Attention: Permissions Coordinator," at the address below.

info@ashleysnotebooks.com
www.ashleysnotebooks.com

www.ingramcontent.com/pod-product-compliance
Lightning Source LLC
LaVergne TN
LVHW081306260125
802193LV00015B/1930

Just 30 minutes a day of slow coloring has been proven to reduce stress and lower blood pressure in the same way your average meditation session would.

WWW.ASHLEYSNOTEBOOKS.COM